SIMPLE Favor
in Ephesians

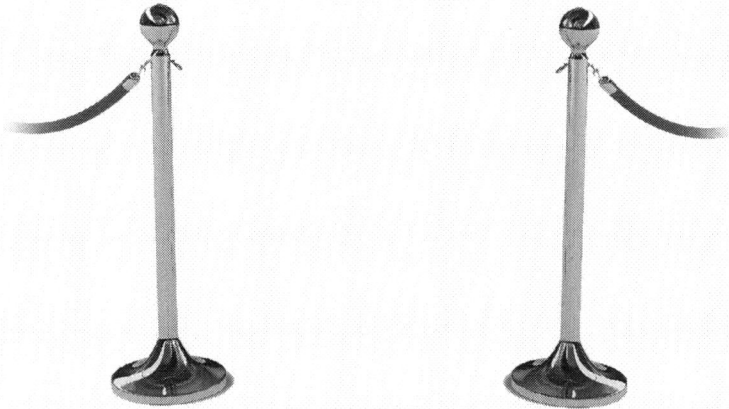

STEVE YOUNG

First Printing, 2015

ISBN-13: 978-1505478143
ISBN-10: 1505478146

Published by: YesBear Publishing
3260 E. Lake Drive
Nashville TN 37214

Cover design: Mark Parq (www.markparq.com)

www.facebook.com/SIMPLEFavorinEphesians
www.facebook.com/SIMPLEWayBooks

www.SIMPLEWayBooks.com

Author available for speaking and coaching

CONTACT INFO:
Steve Young with *Good Tree Life Tools*
steve@GoodTreeLifeTools.com

Contents

Who Will Benefit From This Book?

Those who want to investigate Christianity on their own.

You're not sure what you believe about Christianity. You want a chance to read the Bible with an unbiased eye; to learn straight from the book and not from a person.

Those who feel the Bible is too difficult to understand.

You've been led to believe only the "professionals" can understand what the Bible means. You want to take the intimidation and confusion out of reading it.

Those who have lost the "umph" to their Christian life.

Your spiritual life isn't what it was in days past. You want a guide to help you re-establish your zeal for the simple truths in the Bible.

Those who want to immerse themselves deeply in the Bible one book at a time.

You've read other devotional books before which have helped you grow spiritually. Now, you want to dig deeper into the scriptures to see what you can learn yourself.

What's Significant about *SIMPLE Favor*?

The Greek word for *favor* **is** *charis* **(xáris).**

It is translated in several ways: *grace, favor, thanks, blessing, good works, credit*

Meaning: *kindness, favor, friendship, mercy, gifting*

The word *charis* **is used thirteen times in the New American Standard translation of Ephesians:** 1:2; 1:6; 2:5; 2:7-8; 3:2; 3:7-8; 4:7; 4:29; 6:24

I chose the word *favor* for the title of this book because of the favor God grants us as his children. It's a significant theme throughout the book of Ephesians, though it is often translated *grace*.

Picture a powerful king into whose presence statesmen and leaders of countries petition an audience. Yet the king's own children enter the palace and run past all those in the outer courts to climb up the throne into their daddy's lap. We have this same privilege. We have not earned it, nor do we deserve it; we are merely recipients of our Father's favor because he made us his children. What honor his favor affords!

Why Study Ephesians...For Six Weeks?

Ephesians was originally written to help the individuals in the church know with their minds the facts about salvation. Not only that, Paul, the author, stresses that they were to act on this knowledge so their lives would demonstrate the change which characterizes a new Christian. They were to be transformed into the image of God, so the world could know what God was like. Actually, the meaning of the word "Christian"—"little Christs"—depicts Paul's goal.

It is my hope that as you spend the next six weeks reading through Ephesians, you won't just read the words, but you'll wrestle with the implications these words have for your life. If your lifestyle hasn't changed after six straight weeks in God's Word, something is wrong. The Word of God is compared to a two-edged sword (Heb. 4:12). It is not weak, but powerful, and it should affect your life greatly. Expect, and welcome, the changes that come into your life. May you be a different person in six weeks because you have encountered the living word (John 1:1) within the written word...and that you have obeyed the commands he has given to you.

If you haven't read the Bible much before, the process set down in this book will help you experience something great. It will remove the intimidation you feel about reading the Bible on your own. You can choose one of three levels of intensity, *a la* KFC— *Regular*, *Crispy*, or *Extra-Crispy!*

Regular – Reading Only. Read all the Bible passages indicated each day and then the written commentary. Speak to God before and after for him to show you things about your own life.

Crispy – Reading Plus Writing. Read all the indicated passages and commentary, and then interact with the verses by completing the SIMPLE Way journaling technique. You may want to write down answers to the *Thoughts for Personal Meditation* each day beginning on page 113. Pray before and after as well.

Extra-Crispy – Reading, Writing, & Memorizing – Read the passages and commentary, complete the SIMPLE Way journal section, and memorize the selected verses from each chapter— two each week. See the article *What? Memorize Scripture?* (p.130) for a helpful system. Incorporate prayer in and throughout everything.

After following this guide for six weeks, you will have mastered a process you can use for any book of the Bible. I encourage you to choose another book of the Bible next—perhaps Galatians or Colossians—and spend several weeks using this method for your study. You may want to use a journal I've written for just this sort of process. It's called *My SIMPLE Journal*. See the end of this book for ordering information.

Studying God's words on you own is an amazing process. I promise; it will change your life!

Steve Young

Nashville, Tennessee

February 2015

Suggestions for Your Study

Each week you will work your way through a chapter of Ephesians; six weeks—six chapters. Here are some suggestions to make your time alone with God more meaningful and rich.

- The first day of your study, (I suggest Sunday because normally you'll have more free time that day) you begin your study *read the entire book* of *Ephesians through in a single sitting.* You'll do this again at the beginning of each week. It will take you probably 15-20 minutes. Don't rush; enjoy the reading. Refer to the outline on page 13 as you read the first time. Remember Ephesians was originally a personal letter from a friend to his friends, and did not have chapter divisions and verses until later. This first step will be invaluable for you to understand the complete flow of the book.

- *Pray to God first each day asking for instruction and for your eyes to be open.* You may pray something like this:

  "God, as I read today, show me how to live my life better. Open my eyes to see and believe the truth."

- *Read the chapter of the week each day* (except the first day of the week because you will have just read the entire book!). During week one, you'll read chapter one each day. During week two, chapter two, and so forth. You will see the focal verses of the day's study in the broader context of the whole chapter. After four weeks, you will have read the entire book 18 times!

- *Read again the focal verses for the day* while noting the main idea Paul presents. Don't run too quickly to my comments. Decide on a main theme yourself and pick up any personal lessons you can. You may jot an idea in the *Phrase* section of the SIMPLE Way journal page for the day.

- *Read the commentary.* Consider it one person's ideas designed to give your own thought process a jump start! As you read, pay attention to what God is showing you.

- *Use the SIMPLE Way method to interact with the passage.* Follow all six steps. Don't be afraid of the *Meditation* portion; it could be the most profound of all!

- *End your time in prayer committing to God that you will follow His guidance today.* Find at least one very specific and tangible way you can *act* on what you've learned today.

The SIMPLE Way Journal Pages

"I can't understand the Bible! It's too complicated!" Either you've heard someone say this, or you were the person saying it! The Bible is a love letter written by a Father to His children. The Father doesn't write to confuse His children but rather to instruct them in the best way of life. But for those who have not read the Bible on their own, it can certainly be intimidating. I guarantee this SIMPLE Way method will "de-intimidate" you!

When I read the Bible for myself, I believe God is even in control of what I chose to read in His word that day. I ask myself, "Why did God have me read this today? At this point in my life, what do I need to learn from Him?" He wants you to understand what you're reading more than you do! Listen to Him.

As you begin this 6-week journey through the book of Ephesians, you'll interact profoundly with each section of the book you read. The SIMPLE steps will help in that interaction. We'll use the word "simple" as a guide for the six-step process:

Select
Investigate
Meditate
Phrase
List
Express

*S*elect

Select and write out the verse or parts of a verse that "wow-ed" you! Don't skip this part, and don't just write the reference! Writing out each word will cement God's idea to your mind. And while you are writing, He can give you more insight. Slow down. Write out the Scripture.

*I*nvestigate

What is going on in this text? What does the writer want the original readers to know? Then ask yourself, what is God is saying to you in this Scripture? Write it down in your own words. Ask the Holy Spirit to teach you the truth of His Word.

Meditate

Next, put your pen down for a moment and visualize this truth in your mind. Determine what kind of images will drive home this principle. Draw what is in your mind. You don't have to be an artist; this is only for you!

Phrase

What is the main theme you are understanding today? Write out a phrase or statement which expresses this theme. (Think of a sound bite, or a Facebook quote). This phrase could serve as a caption to the meditation drawing you just completed.

List

List up to three ways to apply the idea to your own life. Personalize what you have read by asking yourself how it applies to your life right now. It may be instruction, encouragement, or a needed correction for you personally.

Express

This step is the most powerful part of the process. Express a written prayer. Share your heart with God. It can be as simple as asking Him to help you live out this Scripture. It might be praising Him for the truth you've learned. It might be a cry for help! Whatever your prayer is this day, write it out.

A SIMPLE Way journal page for your use accompanies each day's reading. You'll find an example on the next page. If you see this page doesn't afford you enough room to write what you'd like, you have several options. You may want to buy a small notebook to use or purchase *My SIMPLE Journal* which I've designed for just this purpose.

Select – *Write out the verse (or part of a verse) you selected.*

Always offering prayer with joy in my every prayer for you all. — v. 4

Investigate – *What do you find in this verse?*

Paul prays frequently for the Philippians using words like "always", "every", and "you all." It's not a once in a while prayer.

Meditate – *What image comes to mind from the passage?*

Phrase – *What is the main theme or statement?*

Paul prays much and often for the Philippians.

List – *Actions you can take because of what you read*

I want to pray every day (and all through the day) for my wife, son, and daughters.

Express – *Write out your prayer to God.*

Lord, thank you that you are so near and always accessible in prayer. Help me to pray each day this week for my family.

The Book of Ephesians

Daily Divisions

OUR WONDERFUL SALVATION — CHAPTERS 1 - 3

Chapter 1: God's Barrage of Blessings

Salvation comes from God and God alone. In addition, the mighty blessings which *accompany* salvation come from him as well. Remember, we are not participants in that salvation process—merely recipients.

A "Pounding" From God (1:1-6)
How Great Is Our Redemption? (1:7-8)
On Purpose or By Accident? (1:9-12)
The Guarantee (1:13-14)
Prayer Power (1:15-18)
A Friend Above All Friends (1:19-21)
The Greatest Gift (1:22-23)

Chapter 2: Dead But Now Alive—Far But Now Near

Prior to this salvation, we were natural humans—apart from a super-natural God. But God changed us from being dead in sin to being alive in righteousness. He transferred us from darkness to light. He brought us from exile into the court of the King.

Dead Guys (2:1-7)
The Gift of Faith (2:8-9)
Remade for a Purpose (2:10)
Disparaging Circumstances (2:11-13)
Know Jesus, Know Jesus; No Jesus, No Peace (2:14-16)
Now You Belong! (2:17-19)
The Amazing Growing Building!?! (2:20-22)

Chapter 3: Mystery & Tribulation

Paul now realizes he has a unique ministry in history. The "big news" is that God wants Gentiles—non-Jews—to be his followers too! For this reason, Paul is greatly persecuted by those who would exclude the Gentiles. He prays for the Ephesians to receive encouragement and even strength through his suffering.

"Fellows" of the Gospel (3:1-6)
The Servant Leader (3:7-10)
That One-Word Question (3:11-12)
The Validation of Trials (3:13)
Praying the "Hard" Stuff (3:14-16)
Supernatural Living (3:17-19)
Beyond Imagination (3:20-21)

OUR WORTHY WALK — CHAPTERS 4 - 6

Chapter 4: Exchanging the Old Life for the New

Paul encourages the Ephesians to work well together within the church—as one body. He says the unconverted Gentiles are self-centered but Christians must change their thinking and act differently. Selflessness is their new life order.

Don't Shoot Your Wounded! (4:1-6)
Your Gift / Others Benefit (4:7, 11-13)
The Great Cultural Exchange (4:8-10)
Difficult Words (4:14-16)
The Re-Thinking Process (4:17-24)
Passive Aggression (4:25-28)
"Sticks and Stones…" (4:29-32)

Chapter 5: A 3-D Picture of God

The reputation of the Christian, who Paul calls the image of God, is very important because the way the Christian lives determines the world's picture of God. Even marriage is an illustration of Christ and his love for his church.

3-D Imaging (5:1-2)
Turning a Deaf Ear (5:3-4)
In The World, But Not of the World (5:5-10)
No Unknown Secrets (5:11-14)
The Wise Walk (5:15-20)
Loving Submission (5:21-24, 33)
Loving Like Christ (5:21, 25-33)

Chapter 6: Relationships & Spiritual Warfare

For the same reason as in chapter five, Christians who are children, parents, slaves (employees), and masters (employers) must live honorable lives. Since we are involved in a spiritual struggle, we must depend on God and his strength to have victory over Satan.

Mutual Responsibility (6:1-4)
Behaving With Authority (6:5-9)
"Turn Around! The Battle's Over There!" (6:10-12)
Holy Armor (6:13-17)
No "Rambos" Allowed (6:18-20)
Trouble and Comfort (6:21-24)
Knowledge and Obedience (Overview of the Book)

Determine in your heart right now to spend time each day over the next six weeks, reading, praying, and searching through the entire book of Ephesians. May this be your prayer:

"Whatever You teach me, Lord, I'll obey."

Week One

Ephesians
Chapter 1

God's Barrage of Blessings

Blessed be the God and Father of our Lord Jesus
Christ, who has blessed us with every spiritual
blessing in the heavenly places in Christ.
(Ephesians 1:3)

I pray that the eyes of your heart may be
enlightened, so that you will know what is the hope
of His calling, what are the riches of the glory of His
inheritance in the saints.
(Ephesians 1:18)

A "Pounding" from God

Read Ephesians in one sitting
Read Focal Passage: Ephesians 1:1-6
Begin memorizing Ephesians 1:3 and 1:18

Write Ephesians 1:3 out in full below.

_____

_____

_____

_____

Once, when we moved from one church staff to another, the ladies of the new church gave us a "pounding." The central idea was to help in the setting up of the kitchen by bringing all the staples we needed in the new home—a "pound" of flour, a "pound" of sugar, and so forth. It was overwhelming for us to see all the grocery bags come into our house filled with gifts from people we hadn't met yet. We had not done anything for these people and were humbled as they treated us so royally.

When we come to Christ, God also gives us a "pounding." He overwhelms us with blessing after blessing—totally undeserved, totally unmatched by our commitment or our obedience.

> *"...who has blessed us in the heavenly realms with every spiritual blessing in Christ"*
> *"...he chose us in him before the creation of the world."*
> *"...he predestined us to adoption to sonship."*
> *"...which he has freely given us in the One he loves."*

The scales of graciousness are tipped in God's favor. We have been inundated by his grace and love. All we can do is accept it and allow ourselves be filled with gratitude.

Select – *Write out the verse (or part of a verse) you selected.*

_____

_____

_____

Investigate – *What do you find in this verse?*

_____

_____

_____

Meditate – *What image comes to mind from the passage?*

Phrase – *What is the main theme or statement?*

_____

_____

List – *Actions you can take because of what you read*

_____

_____

Express – *Write out your prayer to God.*

_____

_____

_____

How Great is Our Redemption?

Read Ephesians 1
Read Focal Passage: Ephesians 1:7-8
Memorize Ephesians 1:3 & 1:18

Write as much as you can of Ephesians 1:3 looking at your Bible as little as possible.

_____

_____

_____

_____

"In accordance with," "according to," "just as must as," "measured just exactly like,"—all these phrases (from different translations of verse 7) mean the same thing. Paul uses this phrase to describe our redemption as compared with "the riches of God's grace."

Just how great is our redemption? To answer this question, we must answer this one: "How great is God's grace?" You see, the answer to both questions is the same. Let's see now...

Think of the most evil person you can possibly imagine. Someone, let's say, who is a hit man—someone who kills people for a living; a bounty hunter for a radical religious sect; someone who even hunts down Christians. Is God's grace immense enough to redeem even a person like this?

Oh, yes! This person even described himself as the "worst" of sinners (1 Tim. 1:15) and yet God reached out with his grace and saved Paul. He transformed this sinner into an apostle called by God.

How great is our salvation? Just as great as God's grace. It is able to save even the foremost of sinners! Oh, what a great salvation!

Select – *Write out the verse (or part of a verse) you selected.*

_____

_____

_____

Investigate – *What do you find in this verse?*

_____

_____

_____

Meditate – *What image comes to mind from the passage?*

Phrase – *What is the main theme or statement?*

_____

_____

List – *Actions you can take because of what you read*

_____

_____

Express – *Write out your prayer to God.*

_____

_____

_____

On Purpose or By Accident?

Day 3 _____

Read Ephesians 1
Read Focal Passage: Ephesians 1:9-12
Memorize Ephesians 1:3 & 1:18

Write out Ephesians 1:3 from memory.

_____

_____

_____

_____

"His will"—"good pleasure"—"purposed"—"predestined"—"plan"—"purpose." All these words and phrases come from this little passage.

In the midst of Paul's description of the great salvation we have in Christ, he unveils God's forethought and planning in the process. My salvation was not happenstance, a mistake, an accident, or an afterthought. Long ago God planned for me to be saved (remember verses 4 & 5?).

My mother loves to give and receive greeting cards. She says, "I know it's not a big thing, but to know that while you were picking out the card you were thinking of me, means a great deal."

I heard the title of a song that is a message in itself, *While He Was On The Cross, I Was On His Mind*. Isn't it great to think that while Jesus was purchasing my salvation, he was thinking of me?

You are not an afterthought or a mistake. God planned long ago the way you would be. Now—what is his purpose…for you?

Select – *Write out the verse (or part of a verse) you selected.*

_____

_____

_____

Investigate – *What do you find in this verse?*

_____

_____

_____

Meditate – *What image comes to mind from the passage?*

Phrase – *What is the main theme or statement?*

_____

_____

List – *Actions you can take because of what you read*

_____

_____

Express – *Write out your prayer to God.*

_____

_____

_____

The Guarantee

Read Ephesians 1
Read Focal Passage: Ephesians 1:13-14
Memorize Ephesians 1:3 & 1:18

Write Ephesians 1:18 out in full below.

_____

_____

_____

_____

The Holy Spirit was given to us at salvation as a pledge—a guarantee—a down payment—assuring us that our inheritance would come. The Holy Spirit alone is a wonderful gift; just think how amazing our inheritance will be!

When asked about heaven, my father-in-law says, "Try to imagine the most wonderful thoughts about heaven possible. Once you've done that, realize that heaven will be far more wonderful than even your wildest dreams."

In the same way, think of the Holy Spirit and how wonderful he is. If He is the down payment, just imagine how amazing our inheritance will be!

During our wedding ceremony, I didn't know I could ever be happier or more in love with my wife than at that moment. Little did I know my love and happiness could grow so much. I have been surprised by how amazing our marriage could be.

Just like salvation, the Holy Spirit is a magnificent gift from God—free and undeserved. We will be pleasantly surprised to find that our inheritance is even greater and will surpass our wildest dreams. "Thanks be to God for his indescribable gift!" (2 Cor. 9:15)

Select – *Write out the verse (or part of a verse) you selected.*

_____

_____

_____

Investigate – *What do you find in this verse?*

_____

_____

_____

Meditate – *What image comes to mind from the passage?*

Phrase – *What is the main theme or statement?*

_____

_____

List – *Actions you can take because of what you read*

_____

_____

Express – *Write out your prayer to God.*

_____

_____

_____

Prayer Power

Day 5 _____

Read Ephesians 1
Read Focal Passage: Ephesians 1:15-18
Memorize Ephesians 1:3 & 1:18

Write as much as you can of Ephesians 1:18 looking at your Bible as little as possible.

_____

_____

_____

_____

The great missionary to China, Jonathan Goforth, was struggling with learning that difficult language. He was on the verge of giving up, when during one sermon, he spoke with more confidence and ability than he ever had before. Several months later, he was amazed to discover that at the very moment he had been preaching, a group of friends in Canada had been praying for him!

In this passage, Paul says he has heard of the great love of the Ephesians. They had a reputation all over the land for such a love. He wanted them to continue in that love and service to God.

For what did he pray for them? Success in ministry? Freedom from trials? Health? No. He prays that they might have wisdom and knowledge, that they would know the "hope" of their calling—the riches of their inheritance.

Prayers of today pale in comparison to prayers in the Bible. We pray often for medical needs, for our house to sell, or for a raise in salary. Why don't we also pray for things of more consequence? For things of a more spiritual nature?

Paul did. Jesus did. We can.

Select – *Write out the verse (or part of a verse) you selected.*

_____

_____

_____

Investigate – *What do you find in this verse?*

_____

_____

_____

Meditate – *What image comes to mind from the passage?*

Phrase – *What is the main theme or statement?*

_____

_____

List – *Actions you can take because of what you read*

_____

_____

Express – *Write out your prayer to God.*

_____

_____

_____

A Friend Above All Friends

Day 6 _____

Read Ephesians 1
Read Focal Passage: Ephesians 1:19-21
Memorize Ephesians 1:3 & 1:18

Write out Ephesians 1:18 from memory.

I used to have a T-shirt that had a bunch of monkeys peeking through some trees. The caption read, "I have friends in HIGH places."

As an eight-year-old boy, I didn't understand the double meaning of the phrase. Having "friends in high place" referred to knowing a lot of people with power—particularly political power. At that age, I was more fascinated with the monkeys!

Look at some of the words in this passage describing God. "Power," "strength," "might," "far above all rule and authority, power and dominion." Our "friend" is in the highest place of all, with the most power.

Think about it. Paul is talking here about the God who, in verse 4, "chose us in him before the creation of the world." The great God of the universe loves me and wants me...and chose me.

Remember: God is not powerless and He loves you with an everlasting love. He wants to be your friend. Let him.

SIMPLE Favor   28

Select – *Write out the verse (or part of a verse) you selected.*

_____

_____

_____

Investigate – *What do you find in this verse?*

_____

_____

_____

Meditate – *What image comes to mind from the passage?*

Phrase – *What is the main theme or statement?*

_____

_____

List – *Actions you can take because of what you read*

_____

_____

Express – *Write out your prayer to God.*

_____

_____

_____

The Greatest Gift

Day 7 _____

Read Ephesians 1
Read Focal Passage: Ephesians 1:22-23
Memorize Ephesians 1:3 & 1:18

Write out both Ephesians 1:3 and 1:18 from memory.

_____

_____

_____

_____

_____

_____

_____

Look closely at verse 22: "[God] appointed Him…for the church." God gave Jesus to the church! His position in the church is one of authority, but his purpose is to be a blessing—a gift—to the church. The result of this gift is that the church—the Christians—might be "filled to the measure of all the fullness of God" (Eph. 3:19).

Here are two quick lessons:

1. Jesus was given as a gift to us and to function as our authority ("head over everything"). Authority over us is not a curse but a blessing. (See also Romans 13:1-4.)

2. Jesus is the head; we are the body. Just like the different parts of our human body are directed by our head, to function correctly, we take our direction from him. To rebel against the head is ludicrous!

Select – *Write out the verse (or part of a verse) you selected.*

_____

_____

_____

Investigate – *What do you find in this verse?*

_____

_____

_____

Meditate – *What image comes to mind from the passage?*

Phrase – *What is the main theme or statement?*

_____

_____

List – *Actions you can take because of what you read*

_____

_____

Express – *Write out your prayer to God.*

_____

_____

_____

Week Two

Ephesians
Chapter 2

Dead But Now Alive—
Far But Now Near

As for you, you were dead
in your transgressions and sins,
in which you used to live
when you followed the ways of this world
and of the ruler of the kingdom of the air,
the spirit who is now at work
in those who are disobedient.
(Ephesians 2:1-2)

For it is by grace you have been saved,
through faith—and this is not from yourselves,
it is the gift of God—not by works,
so that no one can boast.
(Ephesians 2:8-9)

Dead Guys

Read Ephesians in one sitting
Read Focal Passage: Ephesians 2:1-7
Begin memorizing Ephesians 2:1-2 and 2:8-9

Write Ephesians 2:1-2 out in full below.

_____

_____

_____

_____

Do you remember the old pirates' saying, "Dead men tell no tales?" There are a lot of things dead men can't do—breathe, see, or talk.

Paul explains we were all dead in our sin before Christ (v.1). He is the one who has changed us. Look at the phrases in verses 5 and 6. Jesus "made us alive" and "raised us up" and "seated us with him." We (again) are on the receiving end of all of his favor. He does this for His own glory so that he will be praised for all that happens (v.7).

This should cause us to be overwhelmed with gratitude, but also, it should also cause us to be patient with our spiritually "dead" friends and family members. We shouldn't get frustrated with them for acting like "dead people."

When they don't respond favorably to our invitations to Christian gatherings, they're just acting consistently with their natures. Dead people have no desire for spiritual things.

Don't get mad at the blind man because he can't see. Pray for him to receive sight! Pray for God to "raise them up" just as He has for you. Remember, you too used to be blind and dead before God gave you sight and life.

Select – *Write out the verse (or part of a verse) you selected.*

_____

_____

_____

Investigate – *What do you find in this verse?*

_____

_____

_____

Meditate – *What image comes to mind from the passage?*

Phrase – *What is the main theme or statement?*

_____

_____

List – *Actions you can take because of what you read*

_____

_____

Express – *Write out your prayer to God.*

_____

_____

_____

The Gift
of Faith

Day 9 _____

Read Ephesians 2
Read Focal Passage: Ephesians 2:8-9
Memorize Ephesians 2:1-2 and 2:8-9

Write as much as you can of Ephesians 2:1-2 looking at your Bible as little as possible.

_____

_____

_____

_____

Picture this: the door of salvation is locked and the only way to open it is with the key of faith. The only way to get the key of faith is to receive it as a grace gift from God. Not only is salvation a gift from God, but also even the faith to obtain salvation is a gift from him. "You have been saved, through faith—and this [faith] is not from yourselves, [the faith that you've received] is the gift of God" (emphasis added).

Remember the end goal of salvation? It is to demonstrate God's kindness (v. 7) and to glorify him. It is clear here that we are not to receive any credit for our salvation because if we could, we would boast about it (v. 9). Then, in effect, he would be sharing his glory with us.

Think about it. God has offered us salvation. He has given us the faith needed to believe that salvation. Essentially, we are on the receiving end of everything; we bring nothing to the table of salvation. All we can do is accept this lavish gift. Wow!

Select – *Write out the verse (or part of a verse) you selected.*

_____

_____

_____

Investigate – *What do you find in this verse?*

_____

_____

_____

Meditate – *What image comes to mind from the passage?*

Phrase – *What is the main theme or statement?*

_____

_____

List – *Actions you can take because of what you read*

_____

_____

Express – *Write out your prayer to God.*

_____

_____

_____

Ephesians 2

Remade for a Purpose

Read Ephesians 2
Read Focal Passage: Ephesians 2:10
Memorize Ephesians 2:1-2 and 2:8-9

Write out Ephesians 2:1-2 from memory.

_____

_____

_____

_____

In the movie *Les Misérables,* the hero, a thief and an animal of a man, is once shown kindness and his life is changed forever. His heart of stone is replaced with a tender heart of love and goodwill. Instead of selfishly seeking his own good at all costs, he only performs acts of kindness for others, even when his kindness costs him everything.

As we have seen over the past few days' readings, we have been shown the ultimate kindness (v. 7). Also, in that kindness, we have been created anew. God is the re-creator of our beings; he is our maker; the author and perfecter of our faith (Heb. 12:2).

Works of art reflect the character and disposition of the artist. We have been remade by God in the character of Christ, to do the same things he did ("and greater things" according to John 14:12). With our *re*-creation, we have a new purpose: to do good works. Even though good works are not the reason for our salvation (v. 9), they are the result.

Select – *Write out the verse (or part of a verse) you selected.*

_____

_____

_____

Investigate – *What do you find in this verse?*

_____

_____

_____

Meditate – *What image comes to mind from the passage?*

Phrase – *What is the main theme or statement?*

_____

_____

List – *Actions you can take because of what you read*

_____

_____

Express – *Write out your prayer to God.*

_____

_____

_____

Ephesians 2

Disparaging Circumstances

Day 11 _____

Read Ephesians 2
Read Focal Passage: Ephesians 2:11-13
Memorize Ephesians 2:1-2 and 2:8-9

Write Ephesians 2:8-9 out in full below.

_____

_____

_____

_____

"Separate"—"excluded"—"strangers"—"without hope"—"without God." Pretty discouraging, huh?

Imagine an exclusive club with pools, tennis courts, free gourmet food, massages—the works. You would love to be a part of this club, but the requirements are out of your hands. The requirement for being a member demands that you must be a member of the royal family.

You have no hope of being a part of this group. You know neither your parents, nor any of your relatives have royal blood in their veins.

One day, the founder of the club invites you to become a member. You explain that your family heritage excludes you. He says, "Don't worry, I've made arrangements to adopt you as my own flesh and blood!"

You were excluded from life with God—but now you've been adopted by the king (Rom. 8:15)!

SIMPLE Favor   40

Select – *Write out the verse (or part of a verse) you selected.*

_____

_____

_____

Investigate – *What do you find in this verse?*

_____

_____

_____

Meditate – *What image comes to mind from the passage?*

Phrase – *What is the main theme or statement?*

_____

_____

List – *Actions you can take because of what you read*

_____

_____

Express – *Write out your prayer to God.*

_____

_____

_____

Know Jesus, Know Peace
No Jesus, No Peace

Read Ephesians 2
Read Focal Passage: Ephesians 2:14-16
Memorize Ephesians 2:1-2 and 2:8-9

Write as much as you can of Ephesians 2:8-9 looking at your
Bible as little as possible.

_____

_____

_____

_____

    Romeo & Juliet—the Hatfield's & McCoys—the old television show *Bridget Loves Bernie*. A familiar story line: two families who have hated each other for generations now have a son and a daughter who want to be married. The love of the couple is strong enough to overcome the years of inbred hatred between the two families. It is difficult for the couple to express their true love because of the feelings of their families. The endings are different in each story, but in some scenarios, peace is even brought between the families themselves.

    In Paul's day, the animosity between the Jews and the Gentiles was well known and deeply ingrained in their cultures. Jews saw the Gentiles as terribly unclean and to be despised. But love—strong love—brings peace. 1 John 4:18 says "perfect love casts out fear." In this verse we see that "Jesus"—the personification of love itself—"is our peace." After centuries of hatred, he is the one who brought peace between the Jews and the Gentiles. He can (and does) bring peace between people today. He abolishes the "enmity"—the hatred—between men and brings them together as more than friends—as brothers!

SIMPLE Favor   42

Select – *Write out the verse (or part of a verse) you selected.*

_____

_____

_____

Investigate – *What do you find in this verse?*

_____

_____

_____

Meditate – *What image comes to mind from the passage?*

Phrase – *What is the main theme or statement?*

_____

_____

List – *Actions you can take because of what you read*

_____

_____

Express – *Write out your prayer to God.*

_____

_____

_____

Now You Belong!

Read Ephesians 2
Read Focal Passage: Ephesians 2:17-19
Memorize Ephesians 2:1-2 and 2:8-9

Write out Ephesians 2:8-9 from memory.

_____

_____

_____

_____

My brother and I have always been close. Though miles have separated us, our relationship has remained strong. One of my earliest memories is seeing him in my mother's arms after they brought him home from the hospital. I was just 3½ years old.

When you became a Christian, many things changed. One thing you may not have realized is that at the point of salvation, you received many new brothers and sisters because you became a part of "God's household."

You also change cultures. You become a citizen of heaven (Phil. 3:20) instead of a citizen of earth. You are no longer an alien or a stranger in a foreign land. You gain a place to belong…and a purpose for life (Eph. 2:10).

I remember a movie called *A Man Without A Country*. Because of some offense, the hero must leave his own country and all other countries shun him as well. Contrary to this story line, you will never again be without a country, a family, or protection again. You are now a part of God's household.

SIMPLE Favor   44

Select – *Write out the verse (or part of a verse) you selected.*

_____

_____

_____

Investigate – *What do you find in this verse?*

_____

_____

_____

Meditate – *What image comes to mind from the passage?*

Phrase – *What is the main theme or statement?*

_____

_____

List – *Actions you can take because of what you read*

_____

_____

Express – *Write out your prayer to God.*

_____

_____

_____

The Amazing Growing Building!?!

Read Ephesians 2
Read Focal Passage: Ephesians 2:20-22
Memorize Ephesians 2:1-2 and 2:8-9

Write out both Ephesians 2:1-2 and 2:8-9 from memory.

_____

_____

_____

_____

_____

_____

_____

Have you ever heard of a building that could grow? Here, Paul is emphasizing that all Christians are growing together as a building.

The *foundation* is composed of the teachings of prophets. Lesson One: Don't discount the Old Testament scriptures. These are the scriptures Jesus studied as a boy. Learn from them.

The *cornerstone* is Christ himself. The stone around which all other stones are built is Jesus. He is first; he is the model; he is central. Lesson number two is this: We must center our lives around Jesus and nothing else.

The *stones* are being fitted together. They are not off trying to make a building of their own. And the final lesson: Cooperate with other Christians and don't hinder their work. Choose to draw together against the common enemy (Eph. 6:12).

Select – *Write out the verse (or part of a verse) you selected.*

_____

_____

_____

Investigate – *What do you find in this verse?*

_____

_____

_____

Meditate – *What image comes to mind from the passage?*

Phrase – *What is the main theme or statement?*

_____

_____

List – *Actions you can take because of what you read*

_____

_____

Express – *Write out your prayer to God.*

_____

_____

_____

Week Three

Ephesians
Chapter 3

Mystery & Tribulation

Now to him who is able to do
immeasurably more than
all we ask or imagine,
according to his power
that is at work within us,
to him be glory in the church
and in Christ Jesus
throughout all generations,
for ever and ever! Amen.
(Ephesians 3:20-21)

You were taught,
with regard to your former way of life,
to put off your old self,
which is being corrupted by its deceitful desires;
to be made new in the attitude of your minds;
and to put on the new self,
created to be like God
in true righteousness and holiness.
(Ephesians 4:22-24)

"Fellows" of the Gospel

Read Ephesians in one sitting
Read Focal Passage: Ephesians 3:1-6
Begin memorizing Ephesians 3:20-21 and 4:22-24

Write Ephesians 3:20-21 out in full below.

_____

_____

_____

_____

The Jewish people were an exclusive bunch. They were "God's chosen people." They were descendants of Abraham, Isaac, and Jacob. They didn't like the idea of mixing with foreigners. Even the Samaritans—who were like their step-cousins—were shunned by the Jews.

The exclusiveness of the Jews is what makes this proclamation of Paul's so awesome. The great "mystery" of the gospel is that finally salvation was open to non-Jews—to the (ooh, shudder) Gentiles! (Being a Gentile myself, I am very grateful for this mystery!)

Look closely at verse six. Not only is the gospel open to the Gentiles, but they are now to share everything with the Jewish believers. "Fellow-heirs, fellow-members of the body, fellow-partakers of the promise." Gentiles and Jews alike are now "fellows." They can now have "fellow-ship" with one another. No longer can there be considered classes of people, nor especially "classes" of Christians.

An old saying says it well: "The ground is level at the foot of the cross." When we're lying prostrate at His feet, we are all the same size and stature.

Select – *Write out the verse (or part of a verse) you selected.*

_____

_____

_____

Investigate – *What do you find in this verse?*

_____

_____

_____

Meditate – *What image comes to mind from the passage?*

Phrase – *What is the main theme or statement?*

_____

_____

List – *Actions you can take because of what you read*

_____

_____

Express – *Write out your prayer to God.*

_____

_____

_____

The Servant Leader

Read Ephesians 3
Read Focal Passage: Ephesians 3:7-10
Memorize Ephesians 3:20-21 and 4:22-24

Write as much as you can of Ephesians 3:20-21 looking at your Bible as little as possible.

_____

_____

_____

_____

"What biblical character would you most like to meet one day?" Hardly anyone would respond with the name of Paul. It seems Paul intimidates people. To think about sitting and talking with someone who went head-to-head with some of the most intelligent thinkers of his day (Acts 16:16-36) is very threatening. He also wrote one of the best early doctrinal statements of the Christian faith—the book of Romans. Paul was "heady" to say the least.

Not only that, but look at his accomplishments. He and Silas were the first missionaries to take the gospel to the Gentiles. He was stoned, driven out of town, imprisoned, shipwrecked—what a life!

The word "servant" just doesn't seem to fit. How can an "apostle" (pretty exclusive title to say the least) also be a "servant"—or (the more accurate idea for this Greek word) a "slave?"

The leaders of the early church understood that to be good leaders, they needed to emulate the "Model Leader"—Jesus Christ himself. Jesus had redefined the term leader for the disciples; the one who is great must be the servant (Matt. 20:25-28).

Select – *Write out the verse (or part of a verse) you selected.*

_____

_____

_____

Investigate – *What do you find in this verse?*

_____

_____

_____

Meditate – *What image comes to mind from the passage?*

Phrase – *What is the main theme or statement?*

_____

_____

List – *Actions you can take because of what you read*

_____

_____

Express – *Write out your prayer to God.*

_____

_____

_____

That One-Word Question

Read Ephesians 3
Read Focal Passage: Ephesians 3:11-12
Memorize Ephesians 3:20-21 and 4:22-24

Write out Ephesians 3:20-21 from memory.

_____

_____

_____

_____

Many times as a minister, I've been asked the "Why?" question with bitterness, anger, and tears. Even so, I've never had a great answer for this question. Somehow my words seem empty and patronizing as I've sought to ease the pain of the questioner.

However, one truth I've learned has carried me through several of these difficult times—the doctrine of the sovereignty of God. To put it simply, God is most assuredly in control of everything no matter how chaotic it looks from my perspective.

To help me get a handle on this difficult concept, I compare it to similar situations I have had with my children. Sometimes, they ask me the "why?" question when I know that they won't understand my response. They don't have the capacity to understand; they aren't mature enough. In the end, they just have to just trust me. And they can trust me if I've been trustworthy (faithful) in the past.

I don't understand all the "purposes" of God, but I do know God. He's been faithful before and I trust his character enough to know he'll be faithful again. One song says, "I don't know what the future holds, but I know who holds the future." I think that sums it up well.

SIMPLE Favor   54

Select – *Write out the verse (or part of a verse) you selected.*

_____

_____

_____

Investigate – *What do you find in this verse?*

_____

_____

_____

Meditate – *What image comes to mind from the passage?*

Phrase – *What is the main theme or statement?*

_____

_____

List – *Actions you can take because of what you read*

_____

_____

Express – *Write out your prayer to God.*

_____

_____

_____

The Validation of Trials

Day 18 _____

Read Ephesians 3
Read Focal Passage: Ephesians 3:13
Memorize Ephesians 3:20-21 and 4:22-24

Write Ephesians 4:22-24 out in full below.

_____

_____

_____

_____

Paul is very concerned that the Ephesians not stumble because of the things that are happening to him. He is in prison at the moment for preaching the same message that brought salvation to the Ephesians. Now the Ephesians themselves are teaching the same good news as well. It is quite possible they could be imprisoned for the very same thing.

The gospel message, in and of itself, is disturbing to people with its call to surrender and self-sacrifice. The persecution Paul is experiencing is actually the validation of his message. If people had accepted Paul's preaching without being disturbed, it would most likely not have been the true gospel. Instead, he is persecuted and this actually becomes his "glory"—and so also the glory of the Ephesians.

We need to present the good news of God without so much of the religious "baggage" that comes with many of our gospel presentations. Some people are offended more by our method of presentation than by the gospel itself.

The gospel alone is offensive. Make sure that when you are persecuted for sharing the gospel, it is because of the gospel itself and not the way you are presenting it.

Select – *Write out the verse (or part of a verse) you selected.*

_____

_____

_____

Investigate – *What do you find in this verse?*

_____

_____

_____

Meditate – *What image comes to mind from the passage?*

Phrase – *What is the main theme or statement?*

_____

_____

List – *Actions you can take because of what you read*

_____

_____

Express – *Write out your prayer to God.*

_____

_____

_____

Praying the "Hard" Stuff

Day 19 _____

Read Ephesians 3
Read Focal Passage: Ephesians 3:14-16
Memorize Ephesians 3:20-21 and 4:22-24

Write as much as you can of Ephesians 4:22-24 looking at your Bible as little as possible.

_____

_____

_____

_____

"Okay, any prayer requests?" the group leader said as the meeting was winding down for the night. What followed was a hospital report full of terminal and not-so-terminal illnesses. Grandmothers with sickness due to the age of their bodies, children with colds, and so on.

When was the last time you went to a meeting of Christians and someone prayed for their neighbor "to be strengthened with power through his Spirit in the inner man" (3:16)? Many of us (myself included) pray prayers that are not supported "according to the riches of His glory." Our prayers tend to be anemic and faithless. Do we even expect an answer? How can we change our "Bless Aunt Betty" prayers to "power through his Spirit" prayers?

First, we must learn to pray prayers that have to do with more than merely the physical & medical needs of others. Be bold and pray specifically for the spiritual needs of the people you know. And, second, we need to pray for things that stretch our faith—for things only God can do. When He answers this kind of specific prayer, it is obvious to everyone and God is glorified because He has clearly answered them.

SIMPLE Favor

58

Select – *Write out the verse (or part of a verse) you selected.*

_____

_____

_____

Investigate – *What do you find in this verse?*

_____

_____

_____

Meditate – *What image comes to mind from the passage?*

Phrase – *What is the main theme or statement?*

_____

_____

List – *Actions you can take because of what you read*

_____

_____

Express – *Write out your prayer to God.*

_____

_____

_____

Supernatural Living

Day 20 _____

Read Ephesians 3
Read Focal Passage: Ephesians 3:17-19
Memorize Ephesians 3:20-21 and 4:22-24

Write out Ephesians 4:22-24 from memory.

_____

_____

_____

_____

Paul continues to list the things he is praying for the Ephesians. Here he is obviously praying for something that they cannot obtain on their own. Look closely at verses 18 and 19.

He wants them to know "the love of Christ." It's a wonderful goal, but look: he describes this love as one "that surpasses knowledge." The love he wants them to "know" is so immense that their finite minds are not able to comprehend it. They cannot attain this love in their own power.

Does this remind you of another passage? Philippians 4:7 talks about the "peace of God, which transcends all understanding." God's love is so great He wants to give us things which are far above the natural; they are SUPER-natural!

To demonstrate this idea, picture a teacup being filled with a thousand gallons of tea! This illustrates just how God wants us to be "filled to the measure of all the fullness of God."

Select – *Write out the verse (or part of a verse) you selected.*

_____

_____

_____

Investigate – *What do you find in this verse?*

_____

_____

_____

Meditate – *What image comes to mind from the passage?*

Phrase – *What is the main theme or statement?*

_____

_____

List – *Actions you can take because of what you read*

_____

_____

Express – *Write out your prayer to God.*

_____

_____

_____

Beyond Imagination

Day 21 _____

Read Ephesians 3
Read Focal Passage: Ephesians 3:20-21
Memorize Ephesians 3:20-21 and 4:22-24

Write out both Ephesians 3:20-21 and 4:22-24 from memory.

_____

_____

_____

_____

_____

_____

_____

Paul finishes here his three-chapter oration about "Our Wonderful Salvation." After describing how amazing this gift is, he cannot help but break into a glorious doxology about God and all his power.

The main focus of these verses is the magnitude of God's grace—God's favor. Like all Fathers, God's nature is to give gifts to his children. Look at the qualifying words here which describe how much he will, or can, give us. He is "able to do immeasurably more than all we ask or imagine." How great is our father in heaven!

Try this: think of the greatest blessing you could possibly receive. Dream big now! Got it? Okay now, this passage is saying that God's gracious giving is more lavish than anything we could even imagine! What a wondrous God we have!

Select – *Write out the verse (or part of a verse) you selected.*

_____

_____

_____

Investigate – *What do you find in this verse?*

_____

_____

_____

Meditate – *What image comes to mind from the passage?*

Phrase – *What is the main theme or statement?*

_____

_____

List – *Actions you can take because of what you read*

_____

_____

Express – *Write out your prayer to God.*

_____

_____

_____

Week Four

Ephesians
Chapter 4

Exchanging the Old Life
for the New

"In your anger do not sin":
Do not let the sun go down
while you are still angry,
and do not give the devil a foothold.
(Ephesians 4:26-27)

Do not let any unwholesome talk
come out of your mouths,
but only what is helpful
for building others up
according to their needs,
that it may benefit those who listen.
(Ephesians 4:29)

Read Ephesians in one sitting
Read Focal Passage: Ephesians 4:1-6
Begin memorizing Ephesians 4:26-27 and 4:29

Write Ephesians 4:26-27 out in full below.

_____

_____

_____

_____

After Paul has described this new salvation—this wonderful, all-inclusive salvation—he begs us to act like the new creatures we are. Using this verse as an introduction, Paul goes on for three more chapters (the second half of the book of Ephesians) detailing what our lives are to look like after this exchange of old life for new (2:1-7).

He begins in verses 2 to 6 by dealing with the issue of our relationships with other believers. In reference to these relationships, I've heard it said that the army of God is the only group that shoots their wounded! When a fellow-soldier has been attacked by the enemy, Satan and the forces of evil, and has fallen into sin, rather than chastising him for his fall, we need to come quickly to his aid. We must seek to do all we can to build him up again as a fellow-struggler in the faith.

I believe this issue includes denominational lines too. You may not believe exactly the same way as someone in another church, but together we are still part of the body of Christ. Instead of arguing and bickering, let's encourage each other and pray for one another! Who do you know who needs some encouragement from you?

Select – *Write out the verse (or part of a verse) you selected.*

_____

_____

_____

Investigate – *What do you find in this verse?*

_____

_____

_____

Meditate – *What image comes to mind from the passage?*

Phrase – *What is the main theme or statement?*

_____

_____

List – *Actions you can take because of what you read*

_____

_____

Express – *Write out your prayer to God.*

_____

_____

_____

Ephesians 4

Your Gift
Others' Benefit

Read Ephesians 4
Read Focal Passage: Ephesians 4:7, 11-13
Memorize Ephesians 4:26-27 and 4:29

Write as much as you can of Ephesians 4:26-27 looking at your Bible as little as possible.

_____

_____

_____

_____

Spiritual gifts are not given to us by God to be hoarded, but to be used for the good of others. Paul said this earlier in 3:2 when he was talking about "the administration of God's grace that was given to me for you." Yes, it is true that each of us have been given at least one spiritual gift and probably several. These are to be used for the benefit of the entire body of Christ (v. 12).

What if you were given a beautiful painting? Where would you put it—on the wall in the living room or in the closet? What a silly question! Wouldn't you get more joy from it if it were displayed in a prominent place so others could enjoy it as well? It would be ludicrous to let it remain in the closet!

Share your gifts with others. They were given to you for just this purpose. Use them to move toward "unity in the faith" (v. 13). No matter what your gift, remember that you play an important part. An orchestra is not complete without the smallest piccolo.

(In addition to the list here in 4:11, look at Rom. 12:6-8 and 1 Cor. 12:8-10 for more examples of spiritual gifts.)

SIMPLE Favor   68

Select – *Write out the verse (or part of a verse) you selected.*

_____

_____

_____

Investigate – *What do you find in this verse?*

_____

_____

_____

Meditate – *What image comes to mind from the passage?*

Phrase – *What is the main theme or statement?*

_____

_____

List – *Actions you can take because of what you read*

_____

_____

Express – *Write out your prayer to God.*

_____

_____

_____

Ephesians 4

The Great Cultural Exchange

Read Ephesians 4
Read Focal Passage: Ephesians 4:8-10
Memorize Ephesians 4:26-27 and 4:29

Write out Ephesians 4:26-27 from memory.

_____

_____

_____

_____

I have a friend whose grandmother was born to a rich Mexican family just before the Mexican Revolution. After the revolution, they were impoverished and had to move to the United States. They experienced intense culture shock as their family tried to adjust to their lower station and the different lifestyle. They went from the "richest of the rich" to the "poorest of the poor."

I've often thought about the "culture shock" Jesus must have experienced during the incarnation (from *carne*, or "flesh," meaning Jesus took on flesh and blood). Think of it. Jesus…in heaven … could do anything! Whatever his desire, it was granted. Great, right?

Then…the incarnation. Suddenly, he's a helpless baby. He can't eat without help. He needs someone to change his swaddling clothes (first-century Pampers). He gets cold. He cries. He gets a piece of hay from the manger stuck in his ear!

When he descended, he really descended! He exchanged his perfect culture for our imperfect one. And he did it out of love for us. "What a friend we have in Jesus!"

Select – *Write out the verse (or part of a verse) you selected.*

_____

_____

_____

Investigate – *What do you find in this verse?*

_____

_____

_____

Meditate – *What image comes to mind from the passage?*

Phrase – *What is the main theme or statement?*

_____

_____

List – *Actions you can take because of what you read*

_____

_____

Express – *Write out your prayer to God.*

_____

_____

_____

Ephesians 4

Difficult Words

Read Ephesians 4
Read Focal Passage: Ephesians 4:14-16
Memorize Ephesians 4:26-27 and 4:29

Write Ephesians 4:29 out in full below.

_____

_____

_____

_____

The words were difficult to hear...because they were hard words. My boss and I were "having a little talk." He was letting me know about my shortcomings (that's a nice way to say it). I had been less productive than I needed to be. I had put in less effort than I ought. In short, I had been lazy and had not taken responsibility for my work.

Brad was a friend, a brother in Christ...and my boss. I needed correction, and it was his responsibility to give it to me. He was a living model of "speaking the truth in love." His desire was only that I do what I was capable of doing. So, he braved the discomfort and dove into my life.

The incident occurred many years ago. I look on this thirty-minute meeting as a huge turning point in my life. A few weeks later I made my first trip to Mexico; my family and I served as missionaries there for twelve years. Several months after this confrontation, Brad was working for another ministry and out of the direct path of my life for good.

What if he had not spoken to me? What if he'd been "too nice?" Where would I be today? Speaking the truth in love reaps wonderful, unforeseen rewards for the speaker...and the hearer.

Select – *Write out the verse (or part of a verse) you selected.*

_____

_____

_____

Investigate – *What do you find in this verse?*

_____

_____

_____

Meditate – *What image comes to mind from the passage?*

Phrase – *What is the main theme or statement?*

_____

_____

List – *Actions you can take because of what you read*

_____

_____

Express – *Write out your prayer to God.*

_____

_____

_____

Ephesians 4

The Re-Thinking Process

Day 26 _____

Read Ephesians 4
Read Focal Passage: Ephesians 4:17-24
Memorize Ephesians 4:26-27 and 4:29

Write as much as you can of Ephesians 4:29 looking at your Bible as little as possible.

_____

_____

_____

_____

We change our minds about what restaurant we want to eat in, what clothes we want to wear, and what college we want to attend. Here, Paul gives us another reason to change our minds—or change our thinking.

Before we knew Christ, our minds thought in a different way. As the Scripture says, "For as he thinks within himself, so he is" (Prov. 23:7, NASV). The mind is the birthplace for action. If we are able to control our thoughts, we can control our actions.

Several times in Scripture, we are told to pay attention to our thoughts. "Set your minds on things above, not on earthly things" (Col. 3:2). "Have the same mindset as Christ Jesus" (Phil. 2:5). "Do not conform to the pattern of this world, but be transformed by the renewing of your mind" (Rom. 12:2).

I have found that the best way to change my wrong thinking is to replace the "wrong" thoughts with the "right" thoughts found in God's Word. So I memorize Scripture which speaks to my "pet" sins. These Scriptures help focus my mind on Christ and not "earthly things." In this way, I am renewed in the spirit of my mind.

Select – *Write out the verse (or part of a verse) you selected.*

_____

_____

_____

Investigate – *What do you find in this verse?*

_____

_____

_____

Meditate – *What image comes to mind from the passage?*

Phrase – *What is the main theme or statement?*

_____

_____

List – *Actions you can take because of what you read*

_____

_____

Express – *Write out your prayer to God.*

_____

_____

_____

Ephesians 4

Passive Aggression

Read Ephesians 4
Read Focal Passage: Ephesians 4:25-28
Memorize Ephesians 4:26-27 and 4:29

Write out Ephesians 4:29 from memory.

_____

_____

_____

_____

Pacifists are people who stand against participation in violence of any kind—wars, fights, and other forms of violence. They see their non-action as a means of peace.

Passivity in the spiritual arena does not work in the Christian life. To do nothing in our combat against evil allows the "other side" to win. Our "non-participation" gives the devil a foothold.

We have many proactive Scriptures about our war with Satan. "Resist the devil" (James 4:7); "Flee the evil desires of youth" (2 Tim. 2:22). The Bible says we naturally live by following the ways of "the ruler of the kingdom of the air" (Eph. 2:1). Our natural and normal course of life is to do the things which please the devil.

We must actively work toward winning the fight against Satan. It's like swimming upstream. If we stop resisting the current, we will definitely not make progress and will actually be swept downstream by the current.

Jesus said, "Whoever is not with me is against me (Matt. 12:30)." We must not only be careful to "not give the devil a foothold," but we also must take away any footholds which are his already.

SIMPLE Favor   76

Select – *Write out the verse (or part of a verse) you selected.*

_____

_____

_____

Investigate – *What do you find in this verse?*

_____

_____

_____

Meditate – *What image comes to mind from the passage?*

Phrase – *What is the main theme or statement?*

_____

_____

List – *Actions you can take because of what you read*

_____

_____

Express – *Write out your prayer to God.*

_____

_____

_____

Ephesians 4

"Sticks and Stones..."

Read Ephesians 4
Read Focal Passage: Ephesians 4:29-32
Memorize Ephesians 4:26-27 and 4:29

Write out both Ephesians 4:26-27 and 4:29 from memory.

_____

_____

_____

_____

_____

_____

_____

"If you can't say anything nice, don't say anything at all." I'm sure each of us grew up with these words. Our parents tried to implement the principle we find in this passage.

Concerning verse 29, if we obeyed this one scripture, 99% of the relational problems of the world would be solved.

What if everyone you met each day used their words for edification—to build you up instead of tear you down? What if every day you had as your goal to use each of your words to encourage the faith of each person you met? What kind of community would we have if this scripture were fully implemented by every person on the planet? Hmmm....

Select – *Write out the verse (or part of a verse) you selected.*

_____

_____

_____

Investigate – *What do you find in this verse?*

_____

_____

_____

Meditate – *What image comes to mind from the passage?*

Phrase – *What is the main theme or statement?*

_____

_____

List – *Actions you can take because of what you read*

_____

_____

Express – *Write out your prayer to God.*

_____

_____

_____

Ephesians 4

Week Five

Ephesians
Chapter 5

A 3-D Picture
of God

Get rid of all bitterness, rage and anger,
brawling and slander,
along with every form of malice.
Be kind and compassionate to one another,
forgiving each other,
just as in Christ God forgave you.
(Ephesians 4:31-32)

Be very careful, then, how you live—
not as unwise but as wise,
making the most of every opportunity,
because the days are evil.
Therefore do not be foolish,
but understand what the Lord's will is.
(Ephesians 5:15-17)

Read Ephesians in one sitting
Read Focal Passage: Ephesians 5:1-2
Begin memorizing Ephesians 4:31-32 and 5:15-17

Write Ephesians 4:31-32 out in full below.

_____

_____

_____

_____

Imitation is looked down upon. When I was a child, we hated to be called a "copycat." To be original was the goal; to come up with the idea first. Later in my teenage years, we wanted to be individuals—to be unique. Even later in high school, I made an "F" on my senior paper because I didn't understand what "plagiarism" meant. I was punished for imitating.

In this chapter however, Paul takes the other argument. He encourages us to be imitators, but look who he wants us to imitate. The only original in the universe is to be our model. In these verses, Paul begins to explain how to imitate God in several areas of life.

In verse two, he describes the primary characteristic of God: love (see also 1 John 4:7-8). We are to follow our leader and act in love. And like a good leader, God doesn't ask us to do anything that he himself hasn't done already. He demonstrated his love for us in the ultimate way—by dying on the cross for us (John 15:13; Rom. 5:8).

We are to be a three-dimensional image of God and his characteristics—a representation to the world of what he is like. After all, we are his ambassadors (2 Cor. 5:20). The picture we present gives the world a clue about God. We must take this seriously!

S_{elect} – *Write out the verse (or part of a verse) you selected.*

_____

_____

_____

I_{nvestigate} – *What do you find in this verse?*

_____

_____

_____

M_{editate} – *What image comes to mind from the passage?*

P_{hrase} – *What is the main theme or statement?*

_____

_____

L_{ist} – *Actions you can take because of what you read*

_____

_____

E_{xpress} – *Write out your prayer to God.*

_____

_____

_____

Ephesians 5

Turning a Deaf Ear

Read Ephesians 5
Read Focal Passage: Ephesians 5:3-4
Memorize Ephesians 4:31-32 and 5:15-17

Write as much as you can of Ephesians 4:31-32 looking at your Bible as little as possible.

_____

_____

_____

_____

Remember, this whole chapter is about imitating God. The first area of life Paul addresses is how we use our words. Not only the words we speak, but also the words to which we listen must be submitted to God for his approval.

This is one of the hardest areas to control. The tongue is a strong little muscle and can take you places you may not want to go. James warns of the dangers of the tongue in the third chapter of his book (see James 3:1-12). He compares it to the rudder of a ship, a fire, and an untamable animal!

Paul also warns about the topics of conversation in which we take part. All of us have been in situations where we are trapped in a situation where others are telling crude, off-color, or otherwise inappropriate stories. We must think ahead of time about what we can do in these situations. What a shame that even Christians tell stories like these!

We are to be bold with our tongues but careful as well. May we not be ashamed for Jesus to be present in every conversation… because we know he is!

SIMPLE Favor   84

Select – *Write out the verse (or part of a verse) you selected.*

_____

_____

_____

Investigate – *What do you find in this verse?*

_____

_____

_____

Meditate – *What image comes to mind from the passage?*

Phrase – *What is the main theme or statement?*

_____

_____

List – *Actions you can take because of what you read*

_____

_____

Express – *Write out your prayer to God.*

_____

_____

_____

Ephesians 5

In the World, But Not of the World

Read Ephesians 5
Read Focal Passage: Ephesians 5:5-10
Memorize Ephesians 4:31-32 and 5:15-17

Write out Ephesians 4:31-32 from memory.

_____

_____

_____

_____

"Choose your friends wisely." "Bad company corrupts good morals." "If you want to know what someone is like, look at their friends."

Many maxims like these reemphasize the basic message of this passage. Remember, we have come from darkness to light, so we need to be careful how we associate with those who remain in darkness.

Our position must be clear to us...and evident to all others. Those who remain in the darkness desire to pull you back into the same practices you have left.

We are practitioners of righteousness. We are trying to "find out what pleases the Lord" (v. 10). This is the goal for our new life. We must sacrifice anything which stands between progression in holiness and our service to God.

We need to walk a difficult line here. While we must not hide behind our safe walls away from the world, neither should we leave the protection of Christian fellowship to brave the "wild, lost world" for the purpose of evangelism. Somewhere, there is a balance. Let us seek it with spiritual wisdom and discernment.

SIMPLE Favor   86

Select – *Write out the verse (or part of a verse) you selected.*

_____

_____

_____

Investigate – *What do you find in this verse?*

_____

_____

_____

Meditate – *What image comes to mind from the passage?*

Phrase – *What is the main theme or statement?*

_____

_____

List – *Actions you can take because of what you read*

_____

_____

Express – *Write out your prayer to God.*

_____

_____

_____

Ephesians 5

No Unknown Secrets

Read Ephesians 5
Read Focal Passage: Ephesians 5:11-14
Memorize Ephesians 4:31-32 and 5:15-17

Write Ephesians 5:15-17 out in full below.

_____

_____

_____

_____

Remember the secret forts, secret passwords, and the secret handshakes when you were young? Later these were replaced with secrets between friends, secrets about teachers, and secrets from your parents. And even later still: secrets about the pastor, secrets about your neighbor, company secrets, and secrets about your tax return.

Do you see the progression from harmless to dangerous—from gossip to embezzlement? Why so many secrets? Most of the time, things done in secret are wrong—they are sinful. Don't you agree? One psychologist says, "We are only as sick as our secrets."

Certainly, we would all be ashamed if the world knew our secrets. But worse yet, what if God knew about the things we have done (or are still doing) in secret. Look at what verse thirteen says, "Everything exposed by the light becomes visible."

We know there is no darkness for God; he sees everything. He already knows about your "secret" deeds. He knows more about you than you know about yourself. The amazing part? Even though he knows all your secrets—the things you're too ashamed for even your best friends to know—He still loves you. One song says: "He who knows me best, loves me most."

Select – *Write out the verse (or part of a verse) you selected.*

_____

_____

_____

Investigate – *What do you find in this verse?*

_____

_____

_____

Meditate – *What image comes to mind from the passage?*

Phrase – *What is the main theme or statement?*

_____

_____

List – *Actions you can take because of what you read*

_____

_____

Express – *Write out your prayer to God.*

_____

_____

_____

Ephesians 5

The Wise Walk

Day 33 _____

Read Ephesians 5
Read Focal Passage: Ephesians 5:15-20
Memorize Ephesians 4:31-32 and 5:15-17

Write as much as you can of Ephesians 5:15-17 looking at your Bible as little as possible.

_____

_____

_____

_____

Walking wisely isn't easy. It's like trying to exit through the entrance of Disney World. Most people are walking in the opposite direction. It takes fortitude and planning to walk against the flow.

Paul spells out several characteristics of "Wise Walkers" (WW).

1. A WW makes good use of his time (v. 16). Time is a gift of God—we don't earn it. It's not a possession. We can't save it— only spend it. Once it's gone, it's gone.

2. A WW understands the will of God (v. 17). What is the will of God? Part of his will is not doing the bad stuff. The rest God reveals through our talents, individual situations, and (gasp) our desires. As we walk close to Him, He begins to give us new desires that match his desires (Ps. 37:4), then we can do what we desire and actually be walking in God's will.

3. A WW is controlled by the Spirit of God (v. 18), and not by "the spirits" (AKA alcohol or drugs). A WW is careful not to submit his life to anything that can control it other than God.

4. A WW is always giving thanks (v. 20). He realizes that everything he has comes from God, even the things he's earned. All good things come from the Lord (James 1:17).

Select – *Write out the verse (or part of a verse) you selected.*

_____

_____

_____

Investigate – *What do you find in this verse?*

_____

_____

_____

Meditate – *What image comes to mind from the passage?*

Phrase – *What is the main theme or statement?*

_____

_____

List – *Actions you can take because of what you read*

_____

_____

Express – *Write out your prayer to God.*

_____

_____

_____

Ephesians 5

Loving Submission

Write out Ephesians 5:15-17 from memory.

_____

_____

_____

_____

Paul begins this section (5:21-6:9) with the command to "submit to one another" (v. 21). Christians—all Christians—are called to humble servitude. However, wives seem to have always caught this verse in the teeth. Sadly, for many husbands, this is the first (and only) verse in the Bible they've memorized!

Paul compares the marriage relationship to the relationship between Christ and the church. Wives get to play the part of the church. The church is to follow Christ's leadership. We, as the church, are to submit to Christ even when we don't understand or agree. But, He has not banished us to silence, nor forbidden us from asking "why" or even making suggestions.

A healthy marriage works in this way. The wife is to follow the husband's leadership. All the while, she makes suggestions and is involved in the decision-making process. A wise couple works closely with each other using delegation to supplement the weaknesses of one with the strengths of the other.

Wives, view serving your husband as serving Christ. Strange as it sounds, it will cause you to love your husband more!

Select – *Write out the verse (or part of a verse) you selected.*

_____

_____

_____

Investigate – *What do you find in this verse?*

_____

_____

_____

Meditate – *What image comes to mind from the passage?*

Phrase – *What is the main theme or statement?*

_____

_____

List – *Actions you can take because of what you read*

_____

_____

Express – *Write out your prayer to God.*

_____

_____

_____

Ephesians 5

Loving Like Christ

Read Ephesians 5
Read Focal Passage: Ephesians 5:21, 25-33
Memorize Ephesians 4:31-32 and 5:15-17

Write out both Ephesians 4:31-32 and 5:15-17from memory.

_____

_____

_____

_____

_____

_____

_____

_____

The relationship between these two people is so interwoven that nothing can happen to the husband without affecting the wife; after all, they are "one flesh" (v. 31). The responsibilities are interwoven as well. For the wife, submitting to her husband is easier when she knows he loves her as much as his own body (v. 28). For the husband, loving his wife is easier when he knows she respects him (v. 33). When a wife knows her husband loves her and she trusts him, she is able to submit with all her heart.

In addition, the husband is to take responsibility for the spiritual growth of his wife also. His goal is to present her to God as "holy and blameless" (v. 27). Husbands, I dare you to take this challenge to lead your wife and family into a closer relationship with God!

Select – *Write out the verse (or part of a verse) you selected.*

_____

_____

_____

Investigate – *What do you find in this verse?*

_____

_____

_____

Meditate – *What image comes to mind from the passage?*

Phrase – *What is the main theme or statement?*

_____

_____

List – *Actions you can take because of what you read*

_____

_____

Express – *Write out your prayer to God.*

_____

_____

_____

Week Six

Ephesians
Chapter 6

Relationships &
Spiritual Warfare

For our struggle is not against flesh and blood,
but against the rulers,
against the authorities,
against the powers of this dark world
and against the spiritual forces of evil
in the heavenly realms.
(Ephesians 6:12)

And pray in the Spirit on all occasions
with all kinds of prayers and requests.
With this in mind, be alert and
always keep on praying
for all the Lord's people.
Pray also for me, that whenever I speak,
words may be given me so that
I will fearlessly make known
the mystery of the gospel.
(Ephesians 6:18-19)

Mutual Responsibility

Read Ephesians in one sitting
Read Focal Passage: Ephesians 6:1-4
Begin memorizing Ephesians 6:12 and 18-19

Write Ephesians 6:12 out in full below.

_____

_____

_____

_____

One day, my daughter, Stephanie, and I were on a trip to the border of Mexico and Texas. As we were talking, she said, "We have such a great family, Daddy. You and Mama are the best parents I know." This statement was every parent's dream! I answered, "I think our family's great too. Each one of you children is so pleasant to be around." To this, she replied, "Well…you taught us."

Each person in a family has responsibilities. Children are to obey; parents are to discipline and instruct in love. The relationship grows stronger when both parties fulfill these responsibilities.

However, none of us are relieved of responsibilities if the other person doesn't live up to his end of the bargain. We are still to obey God's commands. These are not IF/THEN statements!

The cycle of instruction/obedience/instruction/obedience begins…with instruction. The parents must teach the children how to obey. The parents (and really the fathers) must set the pace for the family and their obedience to God's commands.

These things don't happen accidentally; we must plan for them. We must be proactive about teaching our families to live for Christ. As parents, this must be our definitive purpose.

Select – *Write out the verse (or part of a verse) you selected.*

_____

_____

_____

Investigate – *What do you find in this verse?*

_____

_____

_____

Meditate – *What image comes to mind from the passage?*

Phrase – *What is the main theme or statement?*

_____

_____

List – *Actions you can take because of what you read*

_____

_____

Express – *Write out your prayer to God.*

_____

_____

_____

Ephesians 6

Behaving With Authority

Read Ephesians 6
Read Focal Passage: Ephesians 6:5-9
Memorize Ephesians 6:12 and 18-19

Write as much as you can of Ephesians 6:12 looking at your
Bible as little as possible.

_____

_____

_____

_____

The next time someone says, "Oh, I'm doing well…under the circumstances," say, "Well, what are you doing under there!?!"

Not only are we sometimes "under" circumstances, we are always under authority. No one is free from authority. They may act like it and rebel against authority, but ultimately they must admit it's true.

Authority is a weighty thing. It is an exciting, and yet scary power to wield. It may be used well or abused and there is a fine line between these two possibilities.

The Bible says, "There is no authority except that which God has established" (Rom. 13:1). We must respect all authority, for God uses authority over us to accomplish his purposes (Rom. 13:4). We must respect authority because in so doing we are respecting God himself.

In this same way, authority is on loan from God. Unlike the gift of salvation which we cannot lose, the loan of authority, if used poorly, certainly can be taken from us. Remember, those under your authority have just as much worth in the eyes of God as you have. Treat them well. You both have the same master.

Select – *Write out the verse (or part of a verse) you selected.*

_____

_____

_____

Investigate – *What do you find in this verse?*

_____

_____

_____

Meditate – *What image comes to mind from the passage?*

Phrase – *What is the main theme or statement?*

_____

_____

List – *Actions you can take because of what you read*

_____

_____

Express – *Write out your prayer to God.*

_____

_____

_____

"Turn Around!
The Battle's Over There!"

Read Ephesians 6
Read Focal Passage: Ephesians 6:10-12
Memorize Ephesians 6:12 and 18-19

Write out Ephesians 6:12 from memory.

_____

_____

_____

_____

I used to play a computer game called *Castles*. The idea was to set up your kingdom, protect it, and conquer all the other kingdoms as well. One strategy was to somehow cause two other kingdoms to go to war, and then after the winner's resources had been depleted, attack them and easily take over two kingdoms at once.

We struggle today with many things: health problems, family problems, work problems, money problems relationship problems. See how Paul describes our struggle—"not against flesh and blood." We have been deceived, and we're battling against the wrong enemies.

The real enemy is Satan and his forces. For this type of warfare, we are terribly under-trained. We need weapons and strategies which come from the spiritual realm and not from our own physical one.

We must depend on God for strength, protection, and direction because he already knows the "schemes" of the devil and how to defeat them. We must prepare ourselves for this supernatural type of warfare and not be "unaware" of Satan's methods (2 Cor. 2:11).

Be careful who you battle.

Select – *Write out the verse (or part of a verse) you selected.*

_____

_____

_____

Investigate – *What do you find in this verse?*

_____

_____

_____

Meditate – *What image comes to mind from the passage?*

Phrase – *What is the main theme or statement?*

_____

_____

List – *Actions you can take because of what you read*

_____

_____

Express – *Write out your prayer to God.*

_____

_____

_____

Ephesians 6

Holy Armor

Read Ephesians 6
Read Focal Passage: Ephesians 6:13-17
Memorize Ephesians 6:12 and 18-19

Write Ephesians 6:18-19 out in full below.

_____

_____

_____

_____

Spiritual armor? What's the "real" story anyway? Whatever the specifics, from these verses, we do learn (or are reminded of) several things.

1. We cannot fight this battle against spiritual forces with conventional weapons.
2. We cannot fight it alone without God's help. We are too weak to battle Satan head-to-head.
3. It is a battle against Satan's forces—not just our mind, nature, or bad circumstances.
4. It cannot be a passive battle in which we simply "float" to victory. It must be an active engagement.
5. Spiritual armor has to do with righteous living. (Study on your own "the armor of light" in Romans 13:12 and see also "the weapons of righteousness" in 2 Corinthians 6:7.)

SIMPLE Favor   104

Select – *Write out the verse (or part of a verse) you selected.*

_____

_____

_____

Investigate – *What do you find in this verse?*

_____

_____

_____

Meditate – *What image comes to mind from the passage?*

Phrase – *What is the main theme or statement?*

_____

_____

List – *Actions you can take because of what you read*

_____

_____

Express – *Write out your prayer to God.*

_____

_____

_____

No "Rambos" Allowed

Read Ephesians 6
Read Focal Passage: Ephesians 6:18-20
Memorize Ephesians 6:12 and 18-19

Write as much as you can of Ephesians 6:18-19 looking at your Bible as little as possible.

_____

_____

_____

_____

I think it's interesting that Paul mentions prayer along with all these implements of warfare. Of the pieces of armor mentioned, only the sword of the Spirit (the Bible) has any offensive capabilities; the rest of the armor is for defensive purposes.

In these verses, we see that one of the most powerful offensive weapons we have against Satan and his forces is prayer. Paul puts it here at the end of the list as if he's building up to something he's wanted to say for a while; the climax of a swell of admonition.

His plea is that they would pray for him. He wants them to be in the battle with him by praying on his behalf. Certainly, he prays for himself, but he sees the value and the necessity of having others pray for him as well.

Another great lesson: We cannot win this fight alone. We must have God's help. This help comes from our own fervent prayers and from the prayers of others. We aren't supposed to be Rambo-style commandos, but the army of God! Ask someone to engage the enemy on your behalf through prayer.

Select – *Write out the verse (or part of a verse) you selected.*

_____

_____

_____

Investigate – *What do you find in this verse?*

_____

_____

_____

Meditate – *What image comes to mind from the passage?*

Phrase – *What is the main theme or statement?*

_____

_____

List – *Actions you can take because of what you read*

_____

_____

Express – *Write out your prayer to God.*

_____

_____

_____

Trouble and Comfort

Read Ephesians 6
Read Focal Passage: Ephesians 6:21-24
Memorize Ephesians 6:12 and 18-19

Write out Ephesians 6:18-19 from memory.

_____

_____

_____

_____

In all likelihood, Paul was writing this letter to the Ephesians from a prison in Rome. He didn't include many details about himself or his situation in the letter. However, he was also sending a "human letter"—Tychicus—to fill in the blanks.

He knew the news would be difficult to hear and so he sent a messenger who could comfort them while giving them the bad report. Tychicus had two things on his agenda: (1) to give the bad news and (2) to "comfort their hearts" as one translation says.

Difficult news is always hard to give as well as receive, but if it is coupled with a loving spirit of comfort, it is easier to swallow.

At times, all of us in this world must give bad news to someone. Let us seek to make it a time where we can comfort the receivers at the same time. This is actually a built-in opportunity to minister. Let us take advantage of it.

SIMPLE Favor   108

Select – *Write out the verse (or part of a verse) you selected.*

_____

_____

_____

Investigate – *What do you find in this verse?*

_____

_____

_____

Meditate – *What image comes to mind from the passage?*

Phrase – *What is the main theme or statement?*

_____

_____

List – *Actions you can take because of what you read*

_____

_____

Express – *Write out your prayer to God.*

_____

_____

_____

Ephesians 6

Knowledge and Obedience

Read the entire book of Ephesians
Memorize Ephesians 6:12 and 18-19

Write out both Ephesians 6:12 and 18-19 from memory.

_____

_____

_____

_____

_____

_____

_____

Paul's main desire was bring up the level of the Ephesians' obedience to their level of knowledge. This is why he spent the first three chapters describing what they should know about the salvation they had received. Then the next three chapters, he describes how they should act with regard to this new knowledge.

James 4:17 says, "Anyone, then, who knows the good he ought to do and doesn't do it, sins." Once we know the things to do, we must obey. We can no longer use ignorance as an excuse.

Hopefully, you have discovered several new things over the past few weeks. I hope you have taken advantage of the study of Ephesians by obeying as you learned. Obedience is a difficult habit to start, but it gets easier to maintain with practice and training (Heb. 5:14). May you continue in obedience as you grow in the knowledge of this wonderful salvation!

SIMPLE Favor   110

Select – *Write out the verse (or part of a verse) you selected.*

_____

_____

_____

Investigate – *What do you find in this verse?*

_____

_____

_____

Meditate – *What image comes to mind from the passage?*

Phrase – *What is the main theme or statement?*

_____

_____

List – *Actions you can take because of what you read*

_____

_____

Express – *Write out your prayer to God.*

_____

_____

_____

Ephesians 6

Thoughts for Personal Meditation

"Most of us stumble on the truth all the time. But we just pick ourselves up, brush ourselves off, and proceed as if nothing has happened." – Winston Churchill

The following meditation thoughts will allow you to delve deeper into the passage you've read. Let the Holy Spirit use them to spur on further actions of obedience. Don't let the busy-ness of the day rob you of the truths you've discovered in your time of reflection.

Ephesians One

A "Pounding" from God – 1:1-6
How is your "Gratitude-to-God Meter" registering—weak or strong? Spend some time rehearsing in your mind just how much God has "pounded" you with blessings.

How Great Is Our Redemption? – 1:7-8
Don't think that someone's sin (or your own) is too great to be forgiven. God's grace is greater than our sin. Don't give up on them...or on yourself!

On Purpose or By Accident? – 1:9-12
Spend some time doing a personal inventory of your talents, skills and desires. These things may point to your unique purpose in the work of God's kingdom. Commit to God that you'll follow hard after this purpose.

The Guarantee – 1:13-14
Have you ever wondered about the security of your salvation? Just remember, the Holy Spirit in your life guarantees the

longevity of your salvation. Rest in that and thank Him for such a wonderful salvation!

Prayer Power – 1:15-18

What do you pray about? Physical and temporal things—or the things of heaven? Spend some time analyzing your praying and then...pray for something great!

A Friend Above All Friends – 1:19-21

Think about a time you've felt down or alone. Now, think about how much this powerful God wants to know you. If you had thought about this fact during that time of discouragement, how would your feelings of discouragement have changed?

The Greatest Gift – 1:22-23

Pray for your authorities—your boss, the police, your pastor, your husband. How is God using them to bring you to the fullness of Christ?

Ephesians Two

Dead Guys – 2:1-7

Pray now for your friends who don't know Christ. Pray that God will cause them to have this new life.

The Gift of Faith – 2:8-9

Be humbly grateful for your salvation and for the faith you've received to accept it. Be sure to give God all (not most) of the glory for your salvation.

Remade for a Purpose – 2:10

If you know Christ, you are a new creation (2 Corinthians 5:17) and you have a new purpose. This purpose puts the interests of others before your own (Philippians 2:3-4). Make sure your actions—every day—match your new purpose.

Disparaging Circumstances – 2:11-13

Think for a moment about the life from which you've come. How far did God have to reach for you? Thank Him for adopting you into His family.

Know Jesus, Know Peace—No Jesus, No Peace – 2:14-16

Where are your relational barriers? What dividing walls need to be removed? Between you and whom else does Jesus need to bring peace? Ask Him for this peace today.

Now You Belong! – 2:17-19

Do you sometimes feel alone or unloved—like you don't belong or you have no purpose? Counter the lie with the truths we've seen here and be sure to spread the word to others about being a part of God's household.

The Amazing Growing Building!?! – 2:20-22

Is your life centered around Jesus—not the church, but Jesus the person? If the building is to stand, he must be central. Give Him that place in your life today.

Ephesians Three

"Fellows" of the Gospel – 3:1-6

What Christian groups do you look down upon? Are there some who look down on you? Remember: "The ground is level..."

The Servant Leader – 3:7-10

How can you be a servant-leader? Who has God called you to serve? Find out soon. There's no greater satisfaction than doing what you've been "called" to do!

That One-Word Question – 3:11-12

Rest in this: "God is in control!"

The Validation of Trials – 3:13

Are you persecuted for telling others about Christ? I hope so. Is it because of the gospel itself, or the manner in which you present it? Ask God for wisdom in this area.

Praying the "Hard" Stuff – 3:14-16

Remember 1:15-18? How do you pray...and for what? Are you a "safe" pray-er or a "dangerous" one? I dare you: Pray for something only God can do—something that would give God a lot of glory, then watch expectantly to see what happens!

Supernatural Living – 3:17-19

Have you experienced much of the "fullness of God?" Maybe you're limiting your intake to only what you can understand. Ask God to "blow your mind" and fill you up with His incomprehensible love and the fullness of His Spirit. Dare to live super-naturally!

Beyond Imagination – 3:20-21

Spend some time thinking of some of the blessings you've received. Then dream of some blessings you would like to receive. Pray for them and then watch for the "exceedingly abundant" answer.

Ephesians Four

Don't Shoot Your Wounded! – 4:1-6

Do you have any strained relationships with other Christians? What do you need to do to make it right—ask for forgiveness? Forgive someone else? Do it today. Remember, just like us, they are a part of the same body of Christ.

Your Gift / Others Benefit – 4:7, 11-13
What has God gifted you to do or to be? Are you using your gift(s)? Are you using them to build up—or tear down—the body of Christ? Make some changes today.

The Great Cultural Exchange – 4:8-10
Spend some time thinking of the love Jesus must have had for you for Him to have given up so much. Thank Him for His love. Try to remember His "inconveniences" when you are inconvenienced.

Difficult Words – 4:14-16
"Speaking the truth in love" is a very difficult command—but, oh, so necessary. Who around you needs someone to speak into their lives? Be brave. Just do it. You could change their life.

The Re-Thinking Process – 4:17-24
Any struggle you have can be met by Scripture. Identify one area in which you need to change your thinking. Find three verses which address this area and memorize them. Then, watch as God transforms your mind and your life. (See the appendix called "What? Memorize Scripture?" on page 130.)

Passive Aggression – 4:25-28
Have you been "coasting" in your spiritual life? What have you been doing to actively resist the devil? Are you still renewing your mind? (See yesterday) Act on these thoughts right now.

"Sticks and Stones..." – 4:29-32
Try an experiment. For the next seven days, note how you use your words. In the morning, pray for opportunities to use your words to encourage each person you meet. Note also how they begin to do the same.

Ephesians Five

3-D Imaging – 5:1-2
Think about the image of God you portray to your friends, co-workers, and neighbors. If the only image someone had of God were your life, what would their idea of God be?

Turning a Deaf Ear – 5:3-4
Think for a moment about situations in the future where you could be around inappropriate conversations. Plan now what you will do which will edify (remember 4:29?) and even set the standard for conversations which follow.

In The World, But Not Of The World – 5:5-10
What are your relationships like? Do you have an unhealthy separation from the world? Or are you "flirting" with it? Pray about where the balance is.

No Unknown Secrets – 5:11-14
Think about the things you do in secret. Why are they kept secret...because they're sinful? Give them up today. God already knows about them anyway. Now, thank Him for His everlasting love.

The Wise Walk – 5:15-20
Think: Are you a Wise Walker? What things need to change for you to be one?

Loving Submission – 5:21-24, 33
I know that this seems to only apply to women and wives, but men also need to understand it. What's God saying to you?

Loving Like Christ – 5:21, 25-33
Again, this is directed primarily to husbands, but we all have roles and responsibilities which affect others. Are you living up to those responsibilities?

Ephesians Six

Mutual Responsibility – 6:1-4

How are you doing these things? Are you loving, honoring, and obeying? Are you not exasperating, but rather training and instructing? How, or why not?

Behaving With Authority – 6:5-9

Do you often complain about the authority over you? Do you treat those under your authority with their due respect? Think about the equality you both have under the mutual authority of God. Correct any attitudes or behaviors which need correcting.

"Turn Around! The Battle's Over There!" – 6:10-12

Think about the things with which you struggle daily. Have you been battling them using your own physical methods instead of God's weapons? Commit to using His armor and tactics from now on.

Holy Armor – 6:13-17

Whatever the "real" meaning of spiritual armor/warfare is, we must be involved or we are passive soldiers for the enemy. How are you involved in the fight against wickedness?

No "Rambos" Allowed – 6:18-20

Who are you praying for regularly? Who is praying for you? Write down a list of a few people you could ask to pray for your spiritual life. Then... ask them.

Trouble And Comfort – 6:21-24

Purpose in your heart to give difficult news with a spirit of comfort. Take advantage of every opportunity to minister to others in need.

Meditate on the truths you have learned. Look back through this study and see what things you had planned to do but weren't able to. Purpose in your heart to obey them soon.

Group Study Guide

SIMPLE Favor in Ephesians may be used as a guide for a small group. Here is a suggested outline for the group sessions.

INTRODUCTION WEEK: Preparation & Anticipation

<u>Opening Questions</u>: *Describe a time when you received something you didn't deserve.*

Preparation

(See that each participant has his own book and Bible to use.)

The title of our study is SIMPLE Favor. *Read the description of "favor" from page 5. Can any of you give an example of how God has shown you favor which you haven't deserved?*

<u>Explain</u> the process of the study to the group by reading aloud the *Why Study Ephesians* section on page 6. You may have several participants read around the circle. Afterward, ask if there are any questions.

<u>Say</u>: *Each participant is expected to participate in at least the **reading** portion of the study. Some may choose to include the **writing** portion by answering the SIMPLE Way journaling questions each day beginning on page 00. I encourage you to **memorize** the suggested verses as well. The more interaction you have with the text, the more life change will occur. You are the judge of what you're ready to do; we want this group to be an encouragement for you to reach your personal goal for the study.*

<u>Ask</u>: *Which one of the three levels of intensity do you feel you will choose, and why? **Regular, Crispy, or Extra-Crispy?***

<u>Explain</u> the suggestions for the group by read 8. You may have several read around the circle. Afterward, ask if there are any questions.

Explain the SIMPLE journaling method for the group by reading aloud the *How to Use the SIMPLE Way Journal* section on page 10. You may have several read around the circle. Afterward, ask if there are any questions.

Anticipation

Ask: *Why did you want to participate in a study like this? What is your motivation?*

Ask: *You'll be involved in this study for the next seven weeks. What changes would you like to see in your life as a result of completing this experience?*

Ask: *Explore the possible barriers by describing the one thing that may derail you from completing this study. Are you open to some suggestions from others in the group to help you overcome this barrier?*

See you next week! We'll talk about what you've learned from **Ephesians 1: God's Barrage of Blessings.**

WEEK ONE: God's Barrage of Blessings (Eph. 1)

Assumptions for the group members:
- Everyone has read *Ephesians* once this week
- Everyone has read *Ephesians 1* seven times
- Everyone has read, thought about, and studied *Ephesians 1* piece by piece

Ask these questions for this chapter only:
- What did you think about the **assignment** when you first heard it?
- What was **difficult** about doing the assignments?
- What **surprised** you about doing the assignments?

Reflection Questions:
- What did you learn or were you reminded of about **God**?
- What did you learn or were you reminded of about **yourself**?
- What other **insights** (or questions) did you write down?

Chapter Time:
- Read Ephesians 1, piece by piece, each person taking a section. Read along in your own version; listen for differences in the translations; let's comment on anything interesting that we find.
- Think about the main **themes** of this chapter.
  - What would you **title** this chapter to catch the idea? [Individually write then share with everyone.]
  - Which would you choose to be the **key verse** for the chapter?

Application Questions:
- Who would like to share with the group **any decisions** you have made this week as a result of your study?
- Let's **pray** now specifically for these things to come about.

Preparation for Next Week:
In this first chapter, we've seen *the blessings we've received* through God's granting us his favor. Chapter two will explain just *how far he's brought us* to make us his children.

See you next week! We'll talk about what you've learned from
Ephesians 2: Dead But Now Alive—Far But Now Near.

WEEK TWO: Dead But Now Alive—Far But Now Near (Eph. 2)

Assumptions for the group members:
- Everyone has read *Ephesians* once this week
- Everyone has read *Ephesians 2* seven times
- Everyone has read, thought about, and studied *Ephesians 2* piece by piece

Reflection Questions:
- What did you learn or were you reminded of about **God**?
- What did you learn or were you reminded of about **yourself**?
- What other **insights** (or questions) did you write down?

Chapter Time:
- Let's read through Ephesians 2, piece by piece, each person taking a section. Read along in your own version; listen for differences in the translations; let's comment on anything interesting that we find.
- Take a moment to think about the **themes** of this chapter. Think about the main theme it presents.
  - o What would you **title** this chapter to catch this idea? [Individually write then share with everyone.]
  - o Which would you choose to be the **key verse** for the chapter?

Application Questions:
- Who would like to share with the group **any decisions** you have made this week as a result of your study?
- Let's **pray** now specifically for these things to come about.

Preparation for Next Week:
In this second chapter, we've seen just *how far God's brought us* to make us his children. Chapter three will explain how *God wants all kinds of people* to be in his family.

See you next week! We'll talk about what you've learned from **Ephesians 3: Mystery & Tribulation.**

WEEK THREE: Mystery & Tribulation (Eph. 3)

Assumptions for the group members:
- Everyone has read *Ephesians* once this week
- Everyone has read *Ephesians 3* seven times
- Everyone has read, thought about, and studied *Ephesians 3* piece by piece

Reflection Questions:
- What did you learn or were you reminded of about **God**?
- What did you learn or were you reminded of about **yourself**?
- What other **insights** (or questions) did you write down?

Chapter Time:
- Let's read through Ephesians 3, piece by piece, each person taking a section. Read along in your own version; listen for differences in the translations; let's comment on anything interesting we find.
- Think about the **themes** of this chapter.
  - What would you **title** this chapter to catch this idea? [Individually write then share with everyone.]
  - Which would you choose to be the **key verse** for the chapter?

Application Questions:
- Who would like to share with the group **any decisions** you have made this week as a result of your study?
- Let's **pray** now specifically for these things to come about.

Preparation for Next Week:
You'll see a shift in themes between chapters 3 and 4. Chapters 1-3 are mainly theoretical / theological / mind themes, while chapters 4-6 begin to put feet to the ideas presented. This is why 4:1 begins with "Therefore...". It's like Paul is saying, "Since we know all this, now what are we going to do about it?" In the fourth chapter, we'll see how God would have his children live differently from the rest of the world.

See you next week! We'll talk about what you've learned from
Ephesians 4: Exchanging the Old Life for the New.

WEEK FOUR: Exchanging the Old Life for the New (Eph. 4)

Assumptions for the group members:
- Everyone has read *Ephesians* once this week
- Everyone has read *Ephesians 4* seven times
- Everyone has read, thought about, and studied *Ephesians 4* piece by piece

Reflection Questions:
- What did you learn or were you reminded of about **God**?
- What did you learn or were you reminded of about **yourself**?
- What other **insights** (or questions) did you write down?

Chapter Time:
- Let's read through Ephesians 4, piece by piece, each person taking a section. Read along in your own version; listen for differences in the translations; let's comment on anything interesting we find.
- Take a moment to think about the **themes** of this chapter. Think about the main theme it presents.
  o What would you **title** this chapter to catch this idea? [Individually write then share with everyone.]
  o Which would you choose to be the **key verse** for the chapter?

Application Questions:
- Who would like to share with the group **any decisions** you have made this week as a result of your study?
- Let's **pray** now specifically for these things to come about.

Preparation for Next Week:
In the fourth chapter, we've seen just *how God wants you as his child to be different* from the way you were before. Chapter five will explain how *God's children are actually a reflection* of his character, especially in the area of interpersonal relationships.

See you next week! We'll talk about what you've learned from **Ephesians 5: A 3-D Picture of God.**

WEEK FIVE: A 3-D Picture of God (Ephesians 5)

Assumptions for the group members:
- Everyone has read *Ephesians* once this week
- Everyone has read *Ephesians 5* seven times
- Everyone has read, thought about, and studied *Ephesians 5* piece by piece

Reflection Questions:
- What did you learn or were you reminded of about **God**?
- What did you learn or were you reminded of about **yourself**?
- What other **insights** (or questions) did you write down?

Chapter Time:
- Let's read through Ephesians 5, piece by piece, each person taking a section. Read along in your own version; listen for differences in the translations; let's comment on anything interesting we find.
- Take a moment to think about the **themes** of this chapter. Think about the main theme it presents.
  - What would you **title** this chapter to catch this idea? [Individually write then share with everyone.]
  - Which would you choose to be the **key verse** for the chapter?

Application Questions:
- Who would like to share with the group **any decisions** you have made this week as a result of your study?
- Let's **pray** now specifically for these things to come about.

Preparation for Next Week:
In the fifth chapter, we've seen just how *God's children are actually a reflection* of his character. Chapter six will continue this theme with the family and the workplace, and then stress who our real enemy is and how to conquer him.

See you next week! We'll talk about what you've learned from
Ephesians 6: Relationships & Spiritual Warfare.

WEEK SIX: Relationships & Spiritual Warfare (Ephesians 6)

Assumptions for the group members:
- Everyone has read *Ephesians* once this week
- Everyone has read *Ephesians 6* seven times
- Everyone has read, thought about, and studied *Ephesians 6* piece by piece

Reflection Questions:
- What did you learn or were you reminded of about **God**?
- What did you learn or were you reminded of about **yourself**?
- What other **insights** (or questions) did you write down?

Chapter Time:
- Let's read through Ephesians 6, piece by piece, each person taking a section. Read along in your own version; listen for differences in the translations; let's comment on anything interesting we find.
- Take a moment to think about the **themes** of this chapter. Think about the main theme it presents.
  - What would you **title** this chapter to catch this idea? [Individually write then share with everyone.]
  - Which would you choose to be the **key verse** for the chapter?

Application Questions:
- Who would like to share with the group **any decisions** you have made this week as a result of your study?
- Let's **pray** now specifically for these things to come about.

End of Study Questions:

1. *What was your **main takeaway** from the entire six-week study? What did you learn about **God**? What did you learn about **yourself**?*
2. *What **actions** will you take because of what you've experienced through this study?*
3. *You may choose to continue studying another book of the Bible using this format. **What will you do next?***

What? Memorize Scripture?

Alright, we've all heard the excuse before (as a matter of fact, we've all given this excuse), "I just can't memorize scripture!" You're in luck; I have the answer for that line: Phooey! Poppycock! No way, Jose!

We memorize things all the time. We can't fill up our minds like we fill up a pitcher of water. Our minds expand like a balloon the more we use them. The real problem is…we're just too lazy. Our minds are mush. They're not used to working hard for something.

Memorizing scripture is a spiritual and mental discipline. It's a lot like physical discipline. The more you train your body, the more strong and agile it becomes. In the same way, the more you train your mind, the more alert and responsive it becomes.

Also, as with training your body, better results come from a clear plan. I can help you with that too.

So, put some effort into it. Be purposeful in your spiritual discipline at least as much as you are in your other disciplined activities. Let's give it a try—whadayasay?

Here's a technique I've used for years to learn verses. It takes a little bit of effort in the beginning, but pays huge dividends in the end.

1. Go to the store and buy some lined 3x5 cards (like you have in the recipe box in the kitchen), a metal ring (the kind you can open and close to add more cards), and a hole puncher.
2. Get 3 or 4 cards together, punch a hole through them all in the top left-hand corner, and put the ring through the hole to connect them all into one packet.
3. Write the verse you're memorizing on the first card in this format: reference/verse/reference. It's important to write slowly and neatly (printing is my preference), concentrating on each word as you write it. This is the beginning of the memorization process.

O Ephesians 2:8-9

For by grace you have been saved
through faith; and that not of
yourselves, it is the gift of God; not as
a result of works, that no one should
boast.

Ephesians 2:8-9

4. On the back of the card, write only the reference. Then, once you memorize the verse, you can review by looking only at the reference side. This helps with "cheating." It may seem counter-intuitive but write the reference upside-down on the back. This will allow you to flip the card on the horizontal axis as you review it.

Ephesians 2:8-9

5. Once you have the verse written, begin memorizing the verse from the end to the beginning; one word at a time. "The end to the beginning," you say? Most of us start at the beginning, repeating and memorizing each word in turn, causing us to say the beginning of the verse several times more than the end. So, as we proceed with repeating the memorized verse, it only gets harder as we proceed. If we memorize from the end to the beginning, the reverse is true: as we go from word to word quoting the verse, we proceed from the less repeated words to the more repeated words; thus making it easier as we go along.

6. As you memorize each word, picture that word in your mind before you go to the next one. I like to visualize each word in the same script my elementary teachers used to write new words on the chalkboard; clear, clean white letters on a dark background. Maybe your favorite script is the Sesame Street block letters. Whatever works for you is fine, but visualize each and every word.

7. Memorize the verse word perfect; that's right, every "a," "of," and "the" in its place. This discipline will allow you to stay more focused and clear about the verse. If we memorize it generally, we'll only have a general recollection of the verse, so let's have word perfect memorization as the goal!

8. Carry this card pack with you wherever you go. I review verses while standing in line at the bank. If you put five minutes per day into this activity, plus add a few minutes of "wasted time" that we all have, it will change your life. Guaranteed!

SIMPLE Favor

In Conclusion

When I was in my twenties, I spent considerable time crafting my personal mission statement. It has served as the basis for all my decisions since that time. I've only altered it once in the 20+ years since.

My mission is to cause individuals to grow in their relationship with God through my active encouragement and by modeling a godly lifestyle [since 1993],
...and to influence others indirectly for Christ through something I've developed or someone I've influenced directly [added in 2007].

The book of Ephesians has been special to me for many years. I remember slowly reading and studying through chapter one and being in awe at what God had done for me.

My desire for writing this book, and the others in the SIMPLE Way series, is for the reader to find some of these same awe-inspiring truths and to experience God as I have. Knowing him more intimately will cause you to life a life which others will admire and want to emulate.

I thank God He's put loving supporters into my life for this project. Thanks to my friend Betsy Yarborough, and to my daughter Mary Kathryn for reading for content and typos. Thanks to my son Mark for his many graphic and aesthetic contributions.

Thanks to my wife for life for reading and re-reading the manuscript. Her continual, unswerving support drove me to complete this new project. I love her dearly.

Blessings to you all,

Steve Young
February 2015

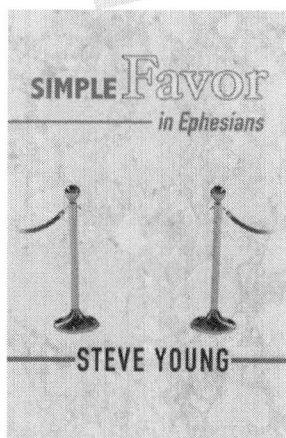

Coming Soon from Simple Way Books!

- SIMPLE Freedom in Galatians
- SIMPLE Harmony in Psalms
- and Other SIMPLE Titles!

Order from
www.SimpleWayBooks.com
Www.Facebook.com/SimpleWayBooks

Made in the USA
Charleston, SC
01 September 2015